Nothing beats a diamond-shaped Holy Grail. G.B. Will, 1966.

Rites of Passage

A CANADIAN RAILWAY RETROSPECTIVE

Greg McDonnell

The BOSTON MILLS PRESS

Cataloguing in Publication Data

McDonnell, Greg, 1954-
Rites of passage: a Canadian railway retrospective

ISBN 1-55046-330-6

1. Railroads – Canada – History – Pictorial works.
2. Railroads – Canada – Trains – History – Pictorial works.
3. Railroads – Canada – History. I. Title.

TF26.M334 2000   385'.0971'09045   00-931785-6

Copyright © 2000 by Greg McDonnell. All rights reserved.

04 03 02 01 00   1 2 3 4 5

Published in 2000 by Boston Mills Press
132 Main Street, Erin, Ontario, Canada N0B 1T0
Tel: 519-833-2407 • Fax: 519-833-2195
e-mail: books@bostonmillspress.com • www.bostonmillspress.com

An affiliate of Stoddart Publishing Co. Limited
34 Lesmill Road, Toronto, Ontario, Canada M3B 2T6
Tel: 416-445-3333 • Fax: 416-445-5967
e-mail: gdsinc@genpub.com

Distributed in Canada by General Distribution Services Limited
325 Humber College Blvd., Toronto, Canada M9W 7C3
Orders: 1-800-387-0141 Ontario & Quebec
Orders: 1-800-387-0172 NW Ontario & other provinces
e-mail: cservice@genpub.com

Distributed in the United States by
General Distribution Services Inc.
PMB 128, 4500 Witmer Industrial Estates
Niagara Falls, New York 14305-1386
Toll-free: 1-800-805-1083 • Toll-free fax: 1-800-481-6207
e-mail: gdsinc@genpub.com • www.genpub.com

Book design by Chris McCorkindale and Sue Breen
McCorkindale Advertising & Design

Printed in Canada

THE CANADA COUNCIL | LE CONSEIL DES ARTS
FOR THE ARTS | DU CANADA
SINCE 1957 | DEPUIS 1957

We acknowledge for their financial support of our publishing
program the Canada Council, the Ontario Arts Council, and
the Government of Canada through the Book Publishing
Industry Development Program (BPIDP).

Front Dust Jacket:
Rust never sleeps. CNR Hamilton, Ontario, October 2, 1975.

Rear Dust Jacket:
Empress Sub tramp, Sceptre, Saskatchewan, September 14, 1999.

Page 1:
Palmerston, Ontario, February 10, 1986.

Page 2:
CP H16-44 8605, Trail, British Columbia, June 24, 1974.

Page 3:
Vaudreuil, Quebec, December 16, 1982.

Page 5:
Boxcars and brakeshoe smoke. CN Extra 9472 East,
Dundas, Ontario, July 7, 1981.

Page 120:
CN Baldur Turn, Ste. Agathe, Manitoba, March 16, 1998.

All photographs by the author unless otherwise noted.

David P. Morgan quotations from August 1957 issue of
TRAINS Magazine appear with the permission of
Kalmbach Publishing Co.

Table of Contents

Essence of a Nation

MANY OF US AMERICAN RAILWAY enthusiasts embrace the conceit that Canada's railways are merely an extension of what we take for granted south of places like Sweet Grass, Sault Ste. Marie, and Rouses Point. This is an understandable character flaw, given the superficial similarities of two nations whose railroads share common operating practices, common suppliers, even common stockholders. It also eloquently explains why generations of American railroad sojourners have treated Canadian Pacific, Canadian National, Algoma Central, and a host of other properties like their own backyard. But—oh, Uncle Sam!—how it misses the mark.

The singular appeal of Canadian railroading gripped me for good ten years ago when, standing on the edge of one of the most bitterly won stretches of Van Horne's mountain railroad, I heard the sound of bagpipes. I was present for the dedication of CPR's audacious new alignment through British Columbia's treacherous Rogers Pass. What better way for the good fathers of CPR to herald their magnificent achievement than to open the proceed-

ings with the Kamloops Pipe Band Society, dressed in full regalia, strutting along a wall of provincial flags, blasting the mesmerizing drone of "Cock O' the North" against the surrounding mountainsides. Anyone with ears knew there was at least one place on Earth where a railway could represent the very essence of nationhood.

That essence is what I believe writer and photographer Greg McDonnell has captured in these remarkable pages: a vision of Canadian railroading as an extension of the Canadian character itself—strong, thoroughgoing, undaunted by natural hardship, mindful of its glorious past. More than perhaps any nation on earth, Canada owes its heritage as a great nation to the ceaseless determination of the people who built and consolidated its railroad empire. It's no accident that Canada's folk singer laureate, Gordon Lightfoot, could turn his elegiac "Canadian Railroad Trilogy" into an international classic (can you imagine Bruce Springsteen getting anywhere near as far with "*American* Railroad Trilogy"?).

But don't take my word for it. Let Greg show you. For the better part of three decades he has turned his formi-

Signals at sunset. East of Galt, Ontario, mileage 50.6, CP Galt Subdivision, September 6, 1990.

Contemplative moments. CPR Bassano at sunset, October 14, 1995.

When I went to college in Michigan some 30 years ago, my friends and I were habitues of the nearby Grand Trunk Western. We hiked its neatly kept right of way, watched its trains from under the eaves of the Durand depot, and just plain fell in love with the sheer "Canadian-ness" of it all. Despite GTW's home address in downtown Detroit, the company's ties to parent Canadian National were as obvious as the maple leafs adorning some of the old freight cars which somehow continued to evade the paint shop. And late at night, I'd lie awake in my dorm room, listening to the melodic horns and the full-throated roar of torpedo-boat GP9's hustling the overnight *International* to Toronto. In the darkness, I imagined the train as it vaulted toward Canada, itself a huge, mysterious presence looming somewhere over the eastern horizon.

Whatever mystery there was about the Canadian railway was long ago solved for me, thanks in large measure to its master storyteller, Greg McDonnell.

Kevin P. Keefe
TRAINS Magazine
Waukesha, Wisconsin
June 2000

dable talents as a writer and photographer to the North American railroad scene. Those skills are on full display here, shining all the more brightly because he has used them to take the full measure of his native land. He's uniquely qualified to explain what is so irresistible about black-and-orange cab diesels, grain trains strung out across a vast prairie, main lines which are truly transcontinental, sport-model 4-8-4's, and that persistent adversary of all railwaymen, the Canadian winter. It's a story as big as a B.C. canyon, as intimate as a quiet night in Spadina roundhouse.

Mindful of the glorious past. Ontario Rail's Credit Valley-lettered ex-CP 4-4-0 136 and Ten-Wheeler 1057
strut through Chatsworth, Ontario, on October 4, 1975, bound for Owen Sound with one of
the group's legendary two-day, doubledheaded steam excursions.

Braced for battle, CP "No. 91 Snowplow," with 1924-built plow 400778, C424 4237, RS18 8742 and van 434401, prepares to depart Orangeville for the Teeswater Sub on February 2, 1977.

Lunch at HO

THE OLD BOXCAR SITS, FADED AND RUSTING on a dead-end track in the CPR's Orangeville, Ontario, yard. Long retired from active duty, the 40-foot grain box has somehow eluded the scrappers and found sanctuary in this lonely yard where the local section crews have commandeered it for material storage. Her reporting marks and number have been obliterated, giving the battered box a degree of anonymity. In fact, it is doubtful that the company even knows that the car exists. For that matter, few, if any, of the hundreds of daily passersby even notice that it's there. For me, though, the forlorn freight car has become an old friend, a touchstone and a symbolic link to so many things that have slipped away.

The section boys may have done their best to conceal her identity, but to those who care enough to look, the old girl is happy to reveal it. It's there, stamped in her side-sill: CP 141378. Look further and her vital statistics and much of her life story are stencilled and otherwise displayed on her weatherbeaten flanks. From the date she was built, "2-54," to her capacity, load limit and empty

Touchstone. CP 141378, HO, January 21, 2000.

weight, "CAPY 133000, LD LMT 133200, LT WT 43800," it's all there, right down to the date of her last overhaul and repainting at Weston shops in Winnipeg: "REPRD WW 3-73, P WW 3-73 GRTN." Cryptic codes and fading dates tell of air-brake maintenance, inspections, and minor repairs performed at Thunder Bay and Toronto Yard; of journals re-packed at Moose Jaw and "DRAFT GEAR

Orangeville, October 24, 1977.

INSPECTED AH 3-4-78." And barely visible beneath 46 years of grit and grease and road dirt caked on her centre-sill is the original stencilling applied by an unknown worker at the time and place of her birth: "NATIONAL STEEL CAR HAMILTON CANADA."

CP 141378. How many times and how many places has that number been typed on waybills, scribbled on switch lists and written in journals and consist reports? How many brakemen have clung to those side ladders, one hand gripping the grab irons, the other waving hand signals or swinging a lantern in the dark? How many carmen have snapped the journal-box covers shut after slaking the thirst of those friction bearings with a slug of journal oil? How many grain doors have been nailed across those

6-foot doorways? How many loads, how many trains? This veteran of 40-some harvests and incalculable millions of miles won't say. However, the patches, welds, scrapes and scars speak volumes.

The years and miles have taken their toll. Her wheels are worn thin, there's a track bolt tack-welded to one of her doors in place of a broken handle, and her rivetted steel body carries the blisters, ripples and wrinkles of age. CP 141378 has most certainly rolled her last mile.

Try as I might, I've never been able to find, in notes or photographs, evidence that I've ever encountered the 141378 in revenue service. Nevertheless, I'd like to think that we've crossed paths somewhere before, perhaps behind the zebra-striped Grand River Railway steeple-cab electrics that trundled past my grandmother's house on Union Boulevard in Kitchener; perhaps on a desolate Saskatchewan branchline, or on a grain train bound for Vancouver, Thunder Bay, or Saint John; perhaps as one of the hundreds of cars I "basic-ed," billed or interchanged to the C&O at Chatham, or on the trains that rattle past our house on Orr's Lake hill.

Whether or not the mystery of past encounters is ever answered, the circumstance of our more recent acquaintance is well known. Blame it on Ralph Carrabs, Jim Brown and Steve Bradley. Ralph owns and operates the Old Train Station restaurant, an establishment housed in the former CPR Orangeville station, which was moved from its original site (exactly where the 141378 now spends its days) to its downtown location in the early 1990s. Brown and

Bradley initiated and maintain the tradition of meeting there for lunch.

Lunch at "HO," as we call it, always referring to the restaurant by its old two-letter CP train-order office signal, has become the custom every few weeks or so. It was en route to one of those lunchtime meetings that I first spotted the 141378 sitting in the yard. Stopping in to visit with the old car has been a part of the Orangeville ritual ever since.

HO is several blocks from the railway now, but the place has retained every bit of its rich history and railroad atmosphere. And, like any self-respecting railway station, it exudes an aura of familiarity and comfort. Even before Kim sets the first pints of Creemore ale on the table, old memories and the spirits of old railroaders come creeping.

I came to be on intimate terms with HO in the summer of 1973, when, as a relief operator, I grudgingly obeyed the written instructions of the London Division Chief Dispatcher: "PLEASE ARRANGE TO PROTECT SECOND HOURS ORANGEVILLE EFFECTIVE JULY 30TH UNTIL FURTHER ADVISED. W.C. BAYNES." Given a choice, I would sooner have stayed at Guelph Junction, where I'd worked for over a month. Compared to the action at GU, the prospects of a sleepy branchline division point were less than appealing.

That changed the first afternoon I walked into the office at HO to relieve the day man, Morley Jaynes. Sure, Orangeville was a shadow of its old self, but the place had character and charm, and the work, what there was of it,

Orangeville bunkhouse, October 24, 1977.

was interesting. My duties on second hours included readying the journal, consist and train orders for the nightly Orangeville–Toronto "Moonlight," exploring the basement, poring over ancient train registers and correspondence, working on a perennially unfinished *TRAINS Magazine* manuscript on CP FA's, and, as Morley explicitly instructed, having a pot of coffee brewed for the Moonlight crew when they came on duty about 2200.

Accommodation was provided in a two-storey bunkhouse, the main floor of which had been a lunch counter in the glory days of full passenger service. Since there were no away-from-home crews assigned there at the time, I had the entire place to myself. For two weeks, it was like living in a time-warp, eating on china marked with the 1930s-era shield of Canadian Pacific Dining Car Service, and sleeping in a bed made with an

Coupled together in the time-honoured tradition, No. 91,
the "Roustabout," and Owen Sound wayfreight No. 71 wait to depart
Orangeville in the rain on August 1, 1973. At Fraxa, the two trains
will part company, with SW1200RS 8147 and the Roustabout
heading for the Teeswater Sub, while RS18 8781 will continue
on to Owen Sound with No. 71.

"Indian blanket" embroidered in Canadian Pacific script.

Each night, after OS-ing the Moonlight, I'd lock up the station, walk over to the bunkhouse, pour a coffee and watch reruns of *The Untouchables* on the black & white TV in the living room, or tune in WABC on the ancient floor-model radio. Eddie Sand, the boomer operator of legendary Harry Bedwell fiction, would have thought he'd died and gone to heaven.

Railroading in Orangeville might have been slow, but it had its moments. Particularly when the crews of the northbound Owen Sound wayfreight and the Teeswater/Walkerton Sub "Roustabout" adhered to the steam-era practice of coupling the two trains together for the assault on the two-percent grade to Fraxa. Often, it was more a matter of necessity than convenience or tradition, as the Roustabout's single SW1200RS, or "pup," as they called it, could handle no more than about 640 tons on the hill to Fraxa. Watching the two trains storm out of town as one—with 8147, a couple cars and a wooden van; RS18 8781, a few more cars and another wooden van—was a sight to behold.

Sitting in Ralph's dining room, the memories come streaming back. From a warm summer night and an unforgettable ride to Toronto on the Moonlight's wooden van—a wild E-ticket ride on CP 438549 with broken springs—to the freezing pre-dawn blackness of a cold January morning, with train crews milling about the waiting room, grips, radios, lanterns and heavy jackets piled on the wooden bench that traces the curved outer wall. It doesn't take much imagination to picture a snow-packed RS3 idling just outside window and hear the offbeat vocals of an Alco 244 marking time while Morley repeats train orders addressed to the "Work Extra 8446 Snowplow."

The Creemore pours, the stories go on and lunch lasts well into mid-afternoon. Cast under HO's captivating spell, it's often difficult to leave...just one more tale of Brown's leverman days at Tecumseh Street, or Peterborough; one more of Bradley's stories of braking out of Revelstoke, or riding No. 1; one more bittersweet account of a roadmaster's last ride. This book was born over those lingering lunches in the old waiting room at HO.

For what it's worth, what follows on these pages is personal—a collection of images and essays drawn from a 35-year effort to capture and chronicle the magic of Canadian railroading; an effort that began with a young boy pointing a borrowed Kodak Brownie at pair of olive-green GMD1's looming out of the early morning fog in Kitchener and quickly grew to be a lifetime avocation, if not vocation.

Railroading has changed immeasurably since that foggy morning 35 years ago. Yet, the essence and emotion remain the same. The camera focuses on the 141378, basking in the low winter sun just yards from the old bunkhouse. Memories of the Moonlight, Indian blankets and *The Untouchables* come rushing in. The shutter releases and tiny gears advance the film. Cold-numbed fingers scrawl details and observations in a dog-eared spiral-bound notebook. Some things haven't changed. This is what it's all about.

Memories of the Moonlight, Indian blankets and
The Untouchables. Orangeville bunkhouse, December 2, 1997.

Spadina sunrise. Coal smoke and clouds of live steam hang in the cold air as CN 4-8-4 6218
eases off the turntable lead at Spadina just after at sun-up on January 24, 1971.

Chapter One

Look Up, Brother—She's Steam!

...we came upon a commuter at Dorval, P.Q, calmly reading his morning paper as Canadian Pacific G-2 4-6-2 No. 2539 strolled past with his train for Montreal and the office. Hastings mused, "Breathes there a man with soul so dead..." and I all but exclaimed, "Look up, brother—she's steam!"

David P. Morgan, TRAINS Magazine

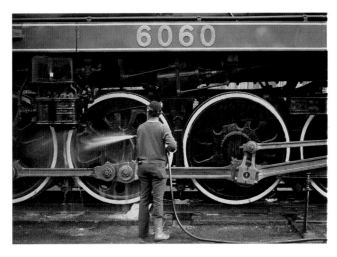

CN 6060, Spadina, May 14, 1974.

THE PROSE IS PURE MORGAN, AND THE passage has been etched in my memory since I first read it as a boy. Forty-some years after D.P.M. banged the words out on his venerable Underwood, they still strike a resonant chord.

Steam. I came late to the party, but not too late—not too late to be awed by CN Northerns and high-stepping, olive-green Hudsons wheeling passenger trains in and out of Kitchener; not too late to watch coal smoke drift past a coach window and listen to the lonesome whistle of the Pacific up front; not too late to witness the gut-wrenching sight of steam scraplines at Stratford, London, Tavistock and Bright.

Steam was dead by the time I was old enough to truly appreciate it. At least it had been pronounced dead. In reality, not all fires were permanently dropped, not all boilers permanently empty. Thanks to benevolent railway management, sympathetic employees and a dedicated, well-connected faction of the faithful, steam still coursed through the cylinders of a select few survivors, if only on certain occasions.

Throughout the 1960s and well into the '70s, steam fantrips, ferry moves and shakedown freight runs provided opportunities to turn back the clock and step into a wonderful world of thumping air compressors, whining turbogenerators, clanking rods and panting exhaust; to savour the intoxicating aroma of hot grease and coal smoke and to revive a boyhood love affair cut short by the efficiencies of internal combustion. Riding on plush walk-over seats and standing at open Dutch doors, I re-lived childhood memories and reveled in experiences of which a boy could only dream: the exhilaration of riding the cab of a Northern making its way from Toronto Union to Spadina on a warm autumn night; the simple pleasure of standing next to a live D10 simmering away the evening in a John Street roundhouse stall; the heart-stopping drama of a freshly overhauled G5 struggling to lift a heavy transfer out of Parkdale, losing its footing on snow-slicked rail before digging in and marching toward Lambton in triumphant glory. If anything, steam was even more captivating in the diesel era. The memories are as vivid as yesterday, and the pulse still quickens at mere mention of numbers 6167, 6218, 6060, 1201, 2860, 1057 and 136. Look up, brother—she's steam!

Homeward bound. CN Passenger Extra 6218 South skirts the shore of Lake Simcoe, south of Orillia, Ontario, at sunset on January 24, 1971.

Spadina slumber. CN 6060, Spadina roundhouse, Toronto, Ontario, September 5, 1977.

Timeless. Deadheading from Toronto to summer excursion service out of Ottawa,
the Ontario Rail Association's ex-CP D10h 4-6-0 1057 and four heavyweight coaches cross
CP's Rideau River bridge at Merrickville, Ontario, on June 29, 1975.

Steam in the snow. Sounding, as D.P.M. said, "like a thousand yesterdays," CP G5a Pacific 1201 storms out of Parkdale Yard with the Toronto Transfer at 1007 on April 26, 1976. Coupled behind the glistening G5, CP RSD17 8921, the transfer's normally assigned engine, is just along for the ride as the 1201 gets a workout on its first shakedown run following shopping at CP's John Street roundhouse. After a pair of break-in runs out of Toronto, the Pacific will move to Ottawa for assignment on NMST's summer excursions between the national capital and Wakefield, Quebec.

Going out in style. Sporting the elephant-ear smoke deflectors of her youth (re-applied for her final season) and making like it's 1945, CNR 4-8-4 6218 storms across the Richelieu River at Beloeil, Quebec, with a Montreal–Richmond fantrip on June 27, 1971.

Richmond, Quebec, June 23, 1974.

Bathed in her own steam, CP 1201 drifts past the coal tower at John Street as she returns to the roundhouse after working a Toronto–Dranoel break-in run on May 16, 1976.

The ivory hunters are on the horizon as H16-44 8711 leads RS18 8785 and GP7 8416
on No. 980 at Yahk, British Columbia, on June 23, 1974.

Chapter Two

Endangered Species

TINY SNOWFLAKES DRIFT SILENTLY THROUGH the glass-less windows of the open cab, settling on broken gauges, torn seats and the rusted backhead of a cold, empty boiler. Secreted in a quiet corner behind CN's Pointe St. Charles shops in Montreal, 0-8-0 8447 is the last of the Mohicans. In December 1967, it is the last unpreserved CNR steam locomotive left on the property.

More than a half-dozen years after dropping its final fire, CN 8447 has somehow escaped the torch. However, the intervening years have not been kind. Its smokebox and boiler-jacket are blistered with rust, and the main rods and valve-gear have been removed. The headlight, marker lights and number glasses are broken out, every pane of window glass has been shattered, and the old engine has been stripped of its number plate, bell, builder's plates, whistle and just about every other removable part.

Efforts to preserve the husky 0-8-0 turned out by the Lima Locomotive Works in June 1923 have failed. Letters pleading with the railway to reconsider have gone unanswered. The 8447 has been sentenced to the same fate

Another H0. CP Train Master 8914 switches at Hochelaga on December 29, 1967.

that befell all but a fortunate few of her sisters, and she'll be billed to the Reclamation Yard in London, Ontario, for scrap.

Standing in the snow just yards away are the moribund hulks of more condemned locomotives. Diesels. Covered with snow and coated with congealed oil and dirt, a line of retired CLC's await their fate. Still dressed in factory-applied mustard-yellow and olive-green paint, CFA16-4's

CP FA1 4019 St. Luc, Quebec

9314 and 9334 are less than 15 years old. Their companions, CN 2900, the road's only Train Master, and passenger C-lines CPA16-5 6704 and CPB16-5 6800, are younger still. Smashed-out number glasses and broken windshields add to the forlorn appearance of the sidelined units, but streaks of oil, like bloodstains on their faded carbodies, under-score the fact that their opposed-piston engines have been forever silenced.

For a kid still struggling to deal with the end of steam, the presence of diesels on death row is disconcerting. Having claimed all but one last straggler, D.P.M.'s mythic ivory hunters have set their sights on new prey. The first—generation diesels that helped kill the fires of the 8447 and thousands of her kind are now endangered themselves.

It is a watershed moment, a moment that sparks an affection for the old and infirm of dieseldom. It is a moment that will inspire a crusade to track down endan-gered diesels across the land. In the spirit of the celebrated steam safaris of another generation, the quest will prompt pilgrimages from coast to coast, from light-rail Maritime branches patrolled by rare RSC13's and RSC24's, to the Kootenay Mountains of British Columbia, where Kingston-built C-lines, H16-44's and Train Masters make their last valiant stand.

In essence, the hunt is kicked-off right there in the snow at the Pointe and begins as Stan Smaill leads the way aboard a succession of Montreal Transit Commission Can-Car and Mack buses that provide passage to CP's Hochelaga Yard in east-end Montreal.

The booming exhaust of a Fairbanks-Morse opposed-piston diesel echoes up the yard as CP Train Master 8914 switches out a cut of cars on the Hochelaga lead. The diamond-shaped CLC builder's plate on her flanks is stamped September 1956, but at age 11, CP H24-66 8914 is already on borrowed time. Indeed, the burly F-M has less than five more months to live, and sisters 8915 and 8919 are already on the deadline at St. Luc.

Oblivious to her impending demise, the great beast soldiers on, digging in to move a cut of cars up the steep grade toward Angus shops. Twenty-four hundred opposed-piston horses bellow out as the engineer notches back the throttle, and the frozen ground quakes as the massive maroon-and-grey machine lumbers past. The kid from smalltown Ontario exposes a few more frames on his very first roll of Kodachrome. The crusade is on. As they will later be at Bridgewater, Charlottetown and Moncton, Nelson, Cranbrook and Crowsnest, ivory hunters are on the horizon.

In classic A-B-B formation, CP FA2 4086 and FB1's 4405 and 4406 thunder up Orr's Lake hill, west of Galt, Ontario, with the westbound OOD ("Double-O D") on June 4, 1974.

Reunion in Charlottetown. CN RSC13 1701, once a regular on the Galt and Elmira wayfreights out of Kitchener, slumbers in the Charlottetown, Prince Edward Island, shop on April 29, 1975.

In the mid-1970s, the Maritime provinces were a Mecca for first-generation diesel rarities. CN's A1A-trucked, 539-engined, 1700-series RSC13's held down assignments on light-rail branches throughout the region and a trio of RSC24's, the only ones in existence, were stabled at Bridgewater, Nova Scotia, for branchline duty. On Prince Edward Island, RSC13's ruled the west side of the island, while the east end was the exclusive domain of CN's last surviving GE 70-tonners.

(Above) On May 2, 1975, CN RSC24 1801 patrols her home turf, trundling through Nictaux Falls, Nova Scotia, with the Bridgewater–Middleton wayfreight.

Ducking beneath the tell-tales, CN 70-tonners 35, 30 and 40 head for the docks at Souris, Prince Edward Island, with potato reefers on April 28, 1975.

With her original Wabash colours showing through, N&W F7A 3671 leads GP7 3453 and a pair of F7 sisters
on a Buffalo–Windsor hotshot, exiting the International Bridge at Fort Erie, Ontario, on July 1, 1972.
The London-built locomotives are among 27 GMD's (22 F7A's, 4 SW8's and 1 GP7) purchased by Wabash for its operations
in southern Ontario, all of which were conducted on CN trackage, exercising rights negotiated with the Grand Trunk in 1898.

CN F7Au 9175, Don Yard, Toronto, Ontario, October 2, 1986.

Engine room, CN 9175, October 2, 1986.

The Train Masters are but a memory, but at the stroke of noon on February 20, 1978, Hochelaga continues to play host to first-generation diesels. Pausing from her switching chores, RS2 8407 waits in the wings as RS10's 8592 and 8598 work past with a transfer bound for St. Luc. All three units were retired in the spring of 1982 and scrapped at Angus shops, just up the hill from HO.

Working the transfer from St. Luc, CP RS10 8590 and RS18 8737 double their train into the yard
at Hochelaga, Quebec, on January 5, 1976.

Stand back. The staccato bark of Alco 251's fills the air on October 26, 1973 as No. 904 thunders past Eastend tower in Chatham, Ontario, behind freshly painted M636 4718 and begrimed sister 4723. White flags gently flapping in the breeze, CP FPA2 4095 stands in the clear with an Extra West that has taken the siding in deference to the hottest train on the London Division.

Mark the date, October 22, 1975. Working a westbound Burlington Turn with SW1200RS 8151, FA2 4089 is the last CP MLW cab to lead a train. Departing Toronto's Lambton Yard on what will be one of its final assignments, the venerable FA passes RSD17 8921 and the morning transfer job. On November 8, the 4089 will be removed from service and shoved onto the ever-lengthening scraplines at St. Luc, never to run again.

Grisly evidence of a violent end, pieces of shattered pistons and broken engine parts litter the gangway of CP RS10 8480 at St. Luc on November 20, 1978.

Reminiscent of scenes from the end of steam, dozens of CP FA's, FB's, RS3's and RS10's, their stacks capped and futures bleak, fill the deadlines at St. Luc, Quebec, on August 24, 1975. While many of the RS3's and RS10's will return to service, the FA's have run their last mile.

Standing where workers once cut up the steam locomotives she helped displace, CN S2 8127
suffers the same fate at the Reclamation Yard in London, Ontario, on March 2, 1975.

Chapter Three

First Snow

"FIRST SNOW NOV-21-81." CHALKED ON the brick wall of the Conrail locomotive shop in St. Thomas, Ontario, the latest in a decade's worth of such notations documents the arrival of winter. In the warmth of the old Canada Southern shop, pigeons coo contentedly and Conrail Geeps quietly await attention. Outside, a bitter north wind rips through the yard, carrying with it, the first significant snow of the season.

According to the calendar, winter does not officially arrive for another month. However, nature abides by her own rules and a full month before the winter solstice, a layer of wet snow blankets the yard and sticks to signals, signs, switch targets and the rusty, rivetted sides of ancient CASO boxcars.

The light dusting of snow is merely a taste of what's to come. But, for the crew of the Conrail "West Local," who have switch brooms at the ready and the cab heaters in GP7 5827 cranked on high, for the sectionmen who shudder at the sight of just a wisp of snow in the switches,

First Snow. Conrail "Canada Southern" shop, St. Thomas, Ontario.

and for the operator in BX Tower, who felt the first signs of frozen resistance in the armstrong levers that control the interlocking's switches, signals and semaphores, it's quite enough. Winter is here, it's in the air, it's in the frozen crunch of snow underfoot, and it's written on the bricks of the CASO shop wall.

Conrail "Canada Southern" shop, St. Thomas, Ontario, January 5, 1981.

Making up their train for Blue Mountain and Nephton, CP FP7 4061, RS10 8599 and RS18 8799
switch at Havelock, Ontario, on February 6, 1978.

Speedometer pegged at a legal mile-a-minute, extra flags stretched taut in the wind, CP SD40 5541, M636 4733 and C424 4206 kick up the fresh-fallen snow as they storm past the stock pens at Ayr, Ontario, with No. 937's freight on December 7, 1976.

Snowbound. CP Owen Sound Sub, south of Owen Sound, Ontario, January 4, 1984.

Northbound on the Owen Sound Sub on January 4, 1984, CP Work Extra 8836 Snowplow slogs through prow-deep snow just south of Owen Sound.

Accelerating into Barrie's Cut, CP Plow Extra 8564 West charges up Orr's Lake hill
west of Galt, Ontario, at 1055, January 24, 1976.

CPR Guelph Jct., Ontario, February 8, 1982

In the midst of a raging blizzard, CP C424 4235 pauses in front of the station at Guelph Jct., Ontario, after running van-hop from London on January 30, 1977. Ordered for snowplow service for three days, the 4235's crew will lift RS10 8561 and a plow at the junction and then fight their way north to Goderich.

Her twin 567B engines howling, CP E8A 1800 churns through pilot-deep snow as she brings
Montreal–Quebec City train No. 154 into Westmount, Quebec, on February 20, 1971.

Huddled in the wooden cab of 1913-vintage spreader 402807, sectionmen deftly manouevre wings and plow blades
to clear the station tracks as CP S3 6524 shoves the ancient Jordan through Montreal West, Quebec, on February 20, 1971.

Approaching the stalling point at about 60 feet per second, CN Work Extra 9178 Snowplow takes a second run at a drifted-over cut north of Hyde Park, Ontario, on January 30, 1978. In a fraction of a second, the crew in the cupola of Jordan-built plow 55614 will know exactly why their seats are outfitted with seatbelts.

The hard way. Sectionmen work to extricate CN Work Extra 9178 Snowplow, stuck in hard-packed drifts at Mileage 14 on the Forest Sub, just east of Lucan, Ontario, on February 1, 1978.

Bearing evidence of a valiant but unsuccessful battle waged with drifts on the line to Goderich, CN 9545 stands in defeat in front of the station at Stratford, Ontario, on December 31, 1976.
In the charge of a trio of GP40-2L's, Stratford–Goderich No. 550 set out into the storm several hours earlier, but 9000 horsepower was no match for Mother Nature. Facing the very real prospect of becoming snowbound on New Years Eve, 550's crew set out their train at Seaforth and retreated to Stratford. Plows will re-open the line come Monday.

Fighting every inch of the way, CP FP7A 4063, assisted by C424 4245 and RS10 8592, struggles through porthole-deep snow with plow 400780, northbound on the St. Marys Sub, at Embro, Ontario, on January 31, 1978.

Undaunted by an early December snowfall, CP M636's 4717 and 4707 stride into Quebec Street yard in London, Ontario, with eastbound hotshot No. 904 on December 10, 1977.

Under a heavy pall of Alco exhaust, ailing CP C424 4223 and RS10 8570 shove Orangeville-assigned plow 400778 into Wingham, Ontario, on January 26, 1982.

Pressed into passenger duty by blizzard conditions, CN SD40 5069 pauses at Stratford, Ontario, with London–Toronto train 666 on January 27, 1978. The SD40, steam generator car and several coaches are substituting for the RDC's normally assigned to this run, but unable to cope with the heavy drifting conditions.

Goodbye, Goderich. Its generator purring the night away, CP van 434447 stands next to the station at Goderich, Ontario, at 15 minutes to midnight, December 15, 1988. Accompanying GP38-2 3032, the Angus-built van has just arrived with the last CP train to Goderich. Come morning, engineer Morris McKenzie and crew will assemble a small train of flatcars loaded with locally built Champion road graders and head south, with the 434447 bringing up the markers as CP exits Goderich for good.

Looking back. Inspection lights on the rear of CP van 434403 probe the darkness as the Aberdeen Turn sifts through fresh-fallen snow on the Goderich Sub, north of Waterdown, Ontario, on February 15, 1990.

First robin, last snow. Conrail "Canada Southern" main line east of St. Thomas, Ontario, April 6, 1982.

Last Snow

HUDDLED AGAINST THE STORM, feathers puffed in an effort to stay warm, a lonely robin sits atop a heavy steel rail while a blustering wind piles snowdrifts across the Canada Southern main east of St. Thomas. Local folklore has it that the arrival of the first robin heralds the coming of spring; indeed, many regard it as a sign of good luck. However, on April 6, 1982, even the talisman is down on his luck. Robins or not, 137 days after an anonymous worker chalked "First Snow" on the wall of the St. Thomas shop, Old Man Winter refuses to relax his grip on the land—at least not without one last blast.

A headlight breaks over the eastern horizon and the robin takes flight. Advancing at about 45 miles per hour, the approaching train disappears every few seconds in great eruptions of snow as C&O GP7 5781 explodes through drift after drift. The world goes white as the Chessie-painted Geep bursts from a bank of drifts just yards away and C&O train CG-41 thunders past in a blizzard of powdery snow and diesel exhaust. From somewhere in the whirling whiteout, an airhorn wails for a distant crossing and hundreds of steel wheels clatter over jointed rail. The commotion begins to fade as the ghostly silhouette of a C&O caboose breezes past and the storm subsides.

As CG-41 disappears in the distance, the robin returns to his perch on the rail and patiently awaits the inevitable arrival of spring.

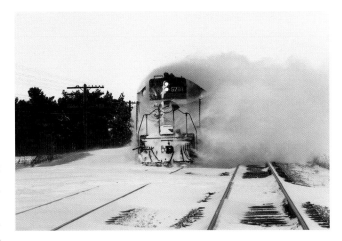

C&O CG-41 driftbusting on the Canada Southern east of St. Thomas, Ontario, April 6, 1982.

Chapter Four

High Iron: To the Horizon and Beyond

I N THE CHILL OF A DYING AUTUMN DAY, THE sinking sun sets the sky ablaze in breathtaking hues of crimson, magenta, azure and gold. The land is silent as lengthening shadows creep quietly across the Alberta prairie, turning pastures and wheatfields from amber to black, turning day into night. Catching the last rays of light, polished steel rails stretch to the horizon and beyond.

Glistening in the twilight on the outskirts of Bassano, the rails are those of the CPR main line, and they extend far beyond the horizon—westward to the Pacific coast, eastward to the Atlantic tidewater.

From out of the east comes the lonely call of a faraway horn and a tiny speck of a headlight appears in the distance. Block signals come to life and sparkle red and green against the darkened sky as a westbound grain train advances across the prairie. The quietude of an October evening dissolves in the two-cycle crescendo of 645-series diesels as CP Extra 9003 West comes trudging through Bassano and grinds to a halt at the west siding switch.

Face to face with a glaring red signal, the 9003 chants impatiently and 114 cars of export grain cool their wheels to meet an eastbound freight. The conductor detrains

Headlight on the horizon. CP Extra 9003 West waits on 492-19 at Bassano, Alberta, October 14, 1995.

Sunset, Bassano, Alberta, October 14, 1995.

CP station, Bassano, Alberta.

and crunches over the ballast to line the siding switch; a headlight materializes, radios crackle and lanterns swing in salute as Montreal-bound manifest 492-14 bears down on Bassano and the 9003.

Headlights dimmed, engines notched down near idle, CP SD40-2 5839 and AC4400CW 9508 weave through the turnout and rumble past with eastbound tonnage. In the warm glow of the 9003's headlight, boxcars and bulkheads loaded with B.C. lumber, multi-level loads of imported autos, piggybacked trailers and double-stacked containers rock and sway down the siding.

The sight of transcontinental traffic passing on the prairie stirs a passion. As Canadians, railroading is our birthright and it is in our blood. This land was built by the railway and is bound together by the steel rails of not one, but two transcontinental railways. To stand at Bassano, or Broadview, or Bala, or Burple, to place one foot on a burnished steel rail and know that it stretches unbroken from ocean to ocean, is to feel a oneness with the nation.

East of Irvine. Heading into a spectacular prairie sunset, CP SD40-2's 5988 and 5987 approach
Irvine, Alberta, with a westbound extra on October 18, 1995.

Kicking up snow and casting lengthy shadows, CN Extra 4124 West rolls past the Manitoba Pool elevator at Mile 10.6, just west of Winnipeg, on February 3, 1981.

The shape of things to come. Operating back to back in classic A-A fashion, CN SD50F 5450 and Dash 8-40CM 2404
wheel Thunder Bay–Coal Valley, Alberta, coal empties past the new Sask Pool high-throughput grain elevator
at Ituna, Saskatchewan, at sunset on July 19, 1996.

Silhouetted against a hazy autumn sky, CP AC4400CW 9528 leads Calgary-bound train 571
west of Redcliff, Alberta, on October 15, 1995.

Twisting through the Box Canyon, Ogden-built CP SD90MAC's 9135 and 9152 work transcontinental hotshot 402-27 east of Revelstoke, British Columbia, on August 27, 1999.

Alco exhaust echoes through woods as CP RS18 8789, RS10 8587 and FPA2 4096 approach
Burple, New Brunswick, with a Saint John-bound grain train on March 9, 1975.

Following the Vueve River, CP SD40 5504, C424 4229, F9B 4473 and GP9 8673 wheel Second 965 over the Cartier Sub near Markstay, Ontario, on February 21, 1975.

Over/under. About to duck under the CP Belleville Sub, eastbound CN GP40-2L's 9450, 9435 and 9439
drift through Beare, Ontario, on June 27, 1975, just as the westbound CP Oshawa Turn,
with RS18's 8763, 8755 and SW1200RS 8168, rolls overhead.

Motown-bound. CP M636's 4718, 4735
and 4704 blast upgrade, tackling Orr's Lake hill
with Montreal–Detroit container train 509
on June 22, 1993.

Dropping down Orr's Lake hill, CP RS18u 1842,
M636 4712 and C424's 4216 and 4233 cruise
through Barrie's Cut, west of Galt, Ontario,
with Second 508 on September 28, 1990.

Skirting the shore of Bedford Basin, VIA FPA4 6782 and F9B 6627 approach Halifax, Nova Scotia, with train No.12, the eastbound *Ocean*, on September 29, 1980.

Highland fling. Speeding toward Truro, Cape Breton & Central Nova Scotia C630M 2039, *William Dunbar*,
sprints over the former-CN Hopewell Sub near Marshy Hope, Nova Scotia, with train No. 407 on June 4, 1994.

Hood doors rattling, traction motors whining and her 660-horsepower 539 engine wound full out,
CN S3 8496, assigned to the afternoon yard job at Kitchener, Ontario, in April 1972,
heads for the East Yard with a string of 40-foot boxcars.

Chapter Five

Intimate Affairs

THE PALPITATING BEAT OF A MᶜINTOSH & Seymour 539 engine reverberated between the brick walls of the H. Krug Furniture factory and the CNR Kitchener station as S3 8497 idled away a cold night in the winter of 1965. The next train wasn't due for an hour or more and the night yard crew wouldn't be on duty until nearly an hour after that. No matter. The comforting chant of the idling S3, the fascinating collection of freight cars in the yard and conversations with the operator and baggageman are enough to enchant the kid who'd trudged a mile and a half through snowy streets just to be there.

That's the thing about railroading. It's more than just trains. For a boy growing up in a small town on a sleepy secondary line, it's a lesson quickly learned. In the hours between trains, there is time to pay attention to detail and to cultivate the art of observation; time to decipher the mysterious codes chalked on car-sides by checkers, brakemen and car-knockers—RIP, SHED, J26, H37— and to consider the slogans painted on off-line cars from faraway places: *Old Reliable, Route of the Hiawathas,*

CN 8469, wooden van 76648 and SW1200RS 1233, Kitchener, Ontario, July 1968.

The Way of the Zephyrs, The Route of the Super Chief All Pullman Chicago–Los Angeles Streamliner; time to study trackwork, date-nails and the simple genius of a No. 10 turnout; time to savor the soft glow of kerosene switch lamps at night and to examine the way the gold-leaf "G.T.R." lettering on the glass of the station clock has peeled and cracked in the decades that have passed since

Framed in the archway of the Kitchener, Ontario, station,
CN S3 8497 idles away a cold January night in 1973.

it marked time between trains led by Moguls, Pacifics and
Mikes lettered Grand Trunk.

What other industry or institution would permit an
outsider, a mere boy at that, to get so close? Close enough
to learn the essence, if not the art, of train-order dis-
patching. Close enough to know every little thing about
the local yard engines (Stratford-assigned CN S3's 8459,
8469, 8496, 8497 and 8498), from the idiosyncrasies of
their non-turbocharged 660-horsepower, in-line 6-cylinder
McIntosh & Seymour 539 engines, to the way their hood
doors shook and rattled when they dug in to lift a heavy
cut of cars; from the variations in paint and other intimate details, to the serial numbers and dates cast in their
bronze MLW builders plates: "80984 JULY 1954." Close
enough to know the insiders—the operators, baggagemen

and sectionmen, brakemen, conductors, engineers and
even the railway constables—by name.

At age 12, the siren call of the world beyond the local
yard limit signs became too strong to resist. Freedom was
a ticket good for unaccompanied passage to Toronto Union
on the red-plush seats of a heavyweight coach drawn by
boiler-fitted B-B GMD1's. Adventure was a day spent on
the railway overpasses at Spadina and Bathurst Street
with a Verichrome Pan-loaded Kodak.

Passenger trains paraded in and out of Union, threading
the maze of crossovers and slip-switches controlled by
John Street Tower; creeping through the hand-throw
switches manned by switchtenders at Bathurst Street and
throttling up past Cabin D. Freights rolled by on the
High Line, and CN and CP S-series switchers shunted on
yard tracks and scooted past with short locals punctuated
by wooden vans carrying kerosene marker lamps. All
the while, burly S13's snorted and barked as they switched
the coach yard and shuttled back and forth to Union with
drafts of passenger equipment. For a smalltown boy, this
was big-time railroading at its best.

Even in the midst of that feverish action, the railroad
was not only accessible, but also remarkably accommo-
dating. Descending from the Spadina bridge, a narrow iron
stairway led directly to the shop tracks and roundhouse.
Calling at the shop foreman's office was a pleasant for-
mality, as the visitor would invariably be granted free
reign to explore the place with a simple admonition: "Just
be careful."

Adhering to that sole proviso kept the welcome mat out at Spadina from that day on. Indeed, Spadina became a very special place. A place to revel in the frenzied activity of a frontline passenger roundhouse, or to quietly wander darkened stalls amid slumbering S2's, FPA4's, Geeps and GMD1's. And Spadina had steam. Not just resident celebrities 6218 and her successor 6060, but steam coursing through radiators and heating pipes throughout the entire complex. Few experiences can compare with that of stepping into the warmth of a steam-heated round-house on a cold winter night.

Spadina was also a place to visit with friends. In the dingy confines of the dingy bunkhouse lunchroom, many memorable hours were spent sharing coffee, beans and conversation with engineers and firemen in from Belleville, Stratford, London and Sarnia.

For the 20 or so years of our acquaintance, Spadina was a comfortable, friendly place that felt like home. And so it remained right up to the very last visit. On a pleasant morning in May 1986, I stopped in at Spadina for the last time. There was no foreman to check in with, no engines on the ready track. I wandered through empty stalls while sparks from cutting torches showered down from above and backhoes clawed at the brick walls of

Cabin D on a rainy night. Bathurst Street, Toronto, Ontario, October 5, 1979.

distant stalls. Even as the place fell under the wrecking ball, no one seemed to mind a visitor—as long as he was careful. Spadina was just like that.

Contemplative moments—on a station platform on a warm night, in the company of a derelict boxcar on a deserted siding, or in the solitude of a darkened round-house stall—it's the quiet moments that add a rich, fulfilling dimension to the railroad experience.

CP 17067

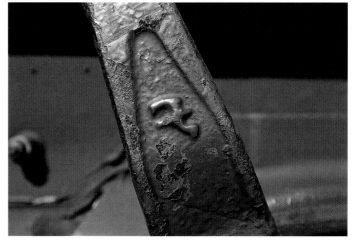

CP 124002

CP 419006

CP 401360

CN 73366

CN 545460

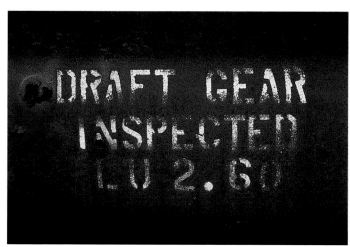

CN 740137

CN 10650

End of the line. CN S4 8157 reposes in a quiet stall at Spadina on May 7, 1974. Retired nearly two years earlier, the 1949-vintage MLW is being cannibalized for parts to keep her Toronto-assigned sisters alive.

Skyscrapers on the Toronto skyline sparkle in the background as FPA4's 6761
and 6777 idle at Spadina on January 3, 1975.

Quitting time, Merriton, Ontario, August 4, 1989.

Making memories. Sault Ste. Marie, Ontario, October 4, 1999.

Rhonda Millar. Swift Current, Saskatchewan, October 16, 1995.

The next generation. Kitchener, Ontario, December 12, 1989.

Reaching deep into the innards of a 539 engine, a shop man works
to change the No. 4 main bearing of CP S3 6545 at John Street
roundhouse in Toronto, Ontario, on February 1, 1983.

Tea time on the Aberdeen Turn. CP 434403,
Flamborough, Ontario, February 15, 1990.

Homeward bound, conductor Ron Bowman tends to paperwork
at his desk aboard CP van 434403, as the Aberdeen Turn
heads back to London, Ontario, on February 15, 1990.

Lights out. Hung out after CP 434049 suffered a generator failure, the tiny red bulb
of a battery lantern substitutes for marker lights as the northbound Aberdeen Turn awaits a signal
at Hamilton Jct., Ontario, on December 15, 1990.

ACR No.3, WC 6636, 3005, 6642, Island Lake, Ontario, October 4, 1999.

Chapter Six

Backwoods, Backroads and Branch Lines

I N THE STILLNESS OF AN OCTOBER DAWN, the haunting call of a solitary loon echoes through the wooded hills north of Sault Ste. Marie. A steamy mist billows from the mirror surface of Upper Island Lake and a frost blankets the land. But for the loon and the occasional scolding of a faraway blue jay, the loudest sound is that of falling leaves.

Under the crystalline layer of frost, steel rails slumber as the first rays of the rising sun ignite the forest in a thousand hues of red, orange, yellow and green. The shadows withdraw and the frost dazzles as it melts in the warmth of the sun.

Carried on the crisp, clear air, the urgent call of an airhorn sounds far to the south. The loon disappears into the mist, the shrieks of the jay and the whispers of falling leaves are quickly drowned out by the howl of approaching EMD's. The Algoma Central is coming alive.

Charging northward, Wisconsin Central SD45 6636, GP40 3005 and SD45 6642 swing through the s-curves

Fall on the Algoma Central, October 4, 1999.

Ken Gonneville at the throttle.

along Island Lake with their turbocharged 645's notched wide open and the Agawa Canyon tour train's 27 sold-out passenger cars hung on their drawbars. Left hand on the throttle, hair blowing in the breeze, engineer Ken Gonneville gives a friendly wave from the cab of the 6636 as he hustles train No. 3 toward Canyon with all of the pomp and urgency of the great Limiteds.

Gonneville's venerable EMD's, of SCL, WP and Santa Fe ancestry, are dressed in Wisconsin Central maroon and cream, but the silver coaches in their wake carry Algoma Central lettering and crests inspired by the line's "Tracks of the Black Bear" slogan. In the case of Wisconsin Central's ACR, these tracks of the black bear are 100-pound rails, rolled in the mills of Algoma Steel and spiked through some of the most spectacular territory on the continent. As backwoods railroading goes, this is as good as it gets.

All the elements of big-time railroading are here, save one—volume. In common with most backwoods roads, branches and secondary lines, traffic and tonnage on the ACR are light. Indeed, after No. 3 clears Island Lake, there will not be another train until late afternoon.

So it is on the branches and backwoods lines from the rocky shores of Cape Breton to the old-growth forests of Vancouver Island. Branch lines, short lines and spun-off regional carriers put up a valiant fight to survive on a diet of low-density traffic. The stakes are high and the consequences steep.

Empty miles of abandoned roadbed, broken fences and vacant bridge abutments that stand like tombstones, bear testament to the lines that have failed. Never more will the picturesque villages of Prince Edward Island hear the call of an airhorn or the clatter of MDT reefers rolling trainloads of spuds to the mainland. Every last mile of Ontario's legendary Bruce Peninsula branchline network has been ripped out and a dozen years have passed since the final O.S. was given in Newfoundland. The last trains have called on hundreds of small towns, from the seaside villages of Prince Edward Island, to backwoods of Vancouver Island.

Those that survive do so with dogged determination and heroic resilience. Invariably, they make up in character and charm what they lack in volume and traffic density. If those values could be inked in the balance sheet, the world would be right.

Approaching Northland, Ontario, with No. 3 on October 4, 1999, Ken Gonneville
unleashes the 10,200 horsepower at his fingertips.

Under the watchful eye of a co-worker, the Electric Lines carman repacks
the journals of CP 437238 at Preston, Ontario, on April 23, 1979.

Ancient timbers groan in protest as the southbound
TH&B Port Maitland local, with GP7 77,
a dozen or so cars and caboose 63, rumble over
a wooden trestle near Port Davidson, Ontario,
on July 17, 1973.

Bridgewater-bound CN RS18's 1777 and 1781 (re-trucked with A1A's from RSC13's) slip through Martin's River, Nova Scotia, with No. 501, on September 29, 1980.

Trundling through the Land of Evangeline, Dominion Atlantic train No. 1, with CP RDC1 9067, crosses the Moose River at Clementsport, Nova Scotia, on April 25, 1975.

Hot and cold on the ACR. The mercury is well below zero Fahrenheit and dropping as Algoma Central Geeps 152 and 171 depart Oba, Ontario, with the southbound Oba Turn at 1545 on February 22, 1976.

Deep in the Agawa Canyon, the temperature is well into the 80s as southbound No. 2,
with a pair of baggage cars, two coaches and business car *Agawa* in the charge of FP9's 1751 and 1750,
passes mileage 116 in the sweltering afternoon heat on June 9, 1997.

Standing in front of CP Electric Lines' Grand River Railway shop at Preston, Ontario, CP 8160 and 8161
wait to go to work on March 9, 1979. Flying white extra flags, 8160 will work the South Job to Brantford and Simcoe,
while sister 8161 will handle the North Job to Waterloo.

Appointed to less demanding chores, CP SW1200RS 8149 looks on as sister 8144—bearing evidence of heavy drifting on the Port Burwell Sub—brings the "Night Tillsonburg" into Woodstock, Ontario, on February 3, 1977.

On the first day of Goderich Exeter operation of the former-CN Goderich and Exeter subdivisions, GEXR GP9 177 switches the waterfront salt mine at Goderich, Ontario, while laid-up lake freighter *Cedarglen* languishes in the harbour on April 6, 1992.

Brad Jolliffe notches back the throttle of Ontario Southland RS18 181 as the ex-CP MLW leads the Guelph Junction Railway local north of Moffat, Ontario, on January 4, 1999. Ontario Southland took over operation of the City of Guelph-owned Guelph–Guelph Junction line from CP in January 1998.

A ritual among fathers and sons for as long as there have been trains.
Mankota, Saskatchewan, August 3, 1998.

Chapter Seven

Prairie Pilgrimage

THE PLACE IS MANKOTA, SASKATCHEWAN. The date is August 3, 1998. The scene is timeless. An old red Fargo pickup rumbles up a gravel road and drifts to a stop at the railway crossing as a trio of CP GP38-2's grind past with a string of grain hoppers. In the truck, a father and four boys—the youngest on the bench seat in the cab, the older ones in the back —look on as the hoppers slowly clump over the crossing. Venturing trackside at train time has been a ritual among fathers and sons for as long as there have been trains.

"They been comin' here a lotta years," the man says, leaning out the window of the old Fargo to talk. There's a poignant undertone to the statement, for we both know that they won't be coming here much longer. The Wood Mountain Subdivision, the 65-mile branch line extending from Ogle to Mankota, will be officially abandoned within weeks. The trains that have been calling on Mankota since 1929 will call no more. The Saskatchewan Pool elevators that have dominated the Mankota skyline for at least that long are likewise doomed. With the loss of the elevators and the railway, the town itself faces an uncertain future.

Heading for Mankota, the Assiniboia Tramp, with CP GP38-2's 3130, 3070 and 3091, grinds upgrade west of Fir Mountain, Saskatchewan, on August 3, 1998. *Andrew McDonnell*

From Mankota to Mendham, Morris and Mortlach, it's the same story in hundreds of small towns across the prairie: elevators closed, branch lines abandoned and the very survival of communities threatened. The country elevator system and branchline network that opened the prairie to agriculture and European civilization is being

Grain and rail. P&H elevator, Mossleigh, Alberta, October 8, 1998.

compelled to ensure that his son sees and experiences a vanishing way of life before it is too late. In this case, the consequences of change are more than just technological.

The changes now sweeping the prairie are far more dramatic than those of previous decades. The effects of dieselization, the disappearance of the passenger train, the closure of railway stations and even branchline rationalization pale in comparison to the virtual disappearance of the country grain elevator and the repercussions thereof. For the most part, when diesels replaced steam, it was simply a matter of the local coming to town behind the usual D10, Pacific, or aging Consol one day and showing up behind a shiny Geep the next. The effects of passenger train discontinuations and station closures were mostly sentimental. It was the elevators on Railway Avenue and the wayfreights that served them that mattered.

Elevator closures and branch line abandonments are epidemic, and rural prairie communities are in crisis. The effects are devastating—and permanent. In an ironic reversal of the nation-building boom at the turn of the previous century, the prairie is in the midst of a wrecking

replaced by centralized "super elevators" and the so-called globalization of the farm economy. In the wake of the economic revolution and in the shadow of concrete, high-throughput terminals are a trail of abandoned branch lines, derelict homesteads and near ghost towns.

For that reason, another father and son have come to watch the GP38's spot empties at the elevators in Mankota. However, unlike the boys in the red Dodge, they have not come from just down the road. They are on a 1500-mile pilgrimage and a mission of some urgency. Just as his own parents did in the waning days of steam, the father is boom. Work crews move across the prairie with cold efficiency, tearing up track, salvaging rail and ties, dismantling bridges and bulldozing buildings. Demolition crews topple elevators and burn the wreckage. They leave nothing behind. Nothing but prairie and sky.

So the father and son move on from Mankato, exploring elevators at Wood Mountain (where the rail in the elevator track—marked "CANADIAN PACIFIC STEEL BLAENAVON 1884"—predates completion of the CPR), Lake Alma, Torquay and Outram; following a quartet of Geeps on a "Dayloader" picking up grain loads from elevators at Killarney, Boissevan, Deloraine and Medora; watching Ron Rasmussen harvest acres of wheat while CN freights roll into the sunset at Dacotah. At Oakner, the Manitoba Pool manager interrupts his work to demonstrate the intricate workings of a country elevator, from lifting grain up the leg to calculating dockage and grading wheat. Over breakfast at a café in Indian Head, Saskatchewan, local farmers discuss the quality of wheat and the quality of life while the sun climbs up the side of the old Paterson elevator. All the while, traffic roars past out on Highway 1 as families in minivans and campers push hard to put the prairie behind them as fast as possible. Oblivious to the economic and cultural revolution that is rapidly altering the landscape and lifestyle of the prairie—as dramatically as the arrival of European settlers did a century earlier—they press on for the mountains. We linger over breakfast in Indian Head, then set out to explore the backroads, branch lines and elevator

towns while there is still time. The Rockies will be there when the son has children of his own.

Assiniboia Tramp, Mankota, Saskatchewan, August 3, 1998.

Heading for the Crow on June 27, 1974, CP Extra 8409 West sprints across the prairie on the
Crowsnest Sub near Cowley, Alberta, with GP7 8409 leading H16-44's 8723 and 8717.

The Rockies loom in the distance as CP van 439515 rolls through the prairie wildflowers,
bringing up the markers of Extra 8409 West, near Cowley, Alberta, on June 27, 1974.

The division between the frozen prairie and the white winter sky is almost imperceptible as CN GP9's 4110 and 4120 race southward on the Letellier Sub near Letellier, Manitoba, on February 17, 1976.

The low winter sun glints off the faded flanks of a tired International farm truck as CP GP38-2 3033 and GP38AC 3011 ease past with the Brooks Wayfreight at Bassano, Alberta, on February 3, 1997.

Tracing the undulating profile of the prairie east of Battrum, Saskatchewan, a perfectly symmetrical train
of grain hoppers glistens in the evening sun as CP GP38-2's 3107 and 3063 work eastbound on the Empress Sub
with 53 loads out of Leader on September 14, 1999.

Framed in the upper window of the old
Alberta Pool Crossfield No. 2 elevator,
CP GP38-2's 3070 and 3033 depart
Crossfield, Alberta, with a northbound
wayfreight on August 26, 1999.

Straining to lift their train after picking up grain loads at the Manitoba Pool elevator,
CP GP38-2 3065, leased LLPX GP60 6002, and CP GP38-2's 3043 and 3080 get on the move
at Medora, Manitoba, at 2025, August 4, 1998.

CN Morris, Manitoba, July 14, 1980.

Returning home after peddling empties on the Miami and Hartney Subs all night long, CN GMD1's 1054 and 1051 pass sisters 1027, 1005 and 1010 on a work train at Margaret, Manitoba, not long after dawn on August 24, 1984.

Southbound on the Three Hills Sub with No. 808, CN Dash 9-44CW 2581 and SD50F 5402 work
the elevator row at Three Hills, Alberta, setting out grain empties on August 25, 1999.

Framed in the skeletal remains of an abandoned shed, CP van 434630 rolls through Sceptre, Saskatchewan, on the rear of the eastbound Empress Sub tramp on September 14, 1999.

The Mendham cat. Mendham, Saskatchewan, September 13, 1999.

Rust never sleeps. Hamilton, Ontario, October 2, 1992.

Chapter Eight

Rust Never Sleeps

CGR initials and vestiges of a cracker box herald. CN 69635, Paris, Ontario, July 4, 1973.

L ANGUISHING IN THE WEEDS, A WORLD WAR One-vintage, CN boxcar decays on a forgotten track in Hamilton, Ontario. Its wood-sheathed sides are weathered grey and almost bare of paint. Patches of moss grow where the wood is sodden and rotting. Rust encrusts the steel underframe, trucks and cast-iron wheels. The rails beneath the car have stratified as they decompose and the ancient steel has taken on a shale-like appearance as it breaks down.

The warm afternoon sun plays on rusted steel, a study in shadow, light, colour and texture that is at once beautiful and disturbing. It's just a rusty wheel on a rusty rail, but the image is compelling.

Maureen calls them "rusty nail shots," these closeup and detail views invariably recorded during meditative moments. Often, a single frame exposed on a rusty nail, or a century-old section of Grand Trunk rail on an overgrown siding, or a spiderweb spun in the cab of a derelict diesel, can say and mean more than an entire roll shot in frantic pursuit of a fast-moving train.

Rusty nail shots. They're pensive views of relics, artifacts and elements of railroading that will soon be gone forever: the broken-out windows of an abandoned station; the stockpiled rail of a ripped-up line; the Canadian Government Railways initials cast in the truck frames of an ancient sleeping car that has rolled its last mile and waits only to be set afire, gutted and cut up for scrap. Inspired by the lessons learned on the steam scraplines in Stratford and amid condemned CLC's in the London Reclamation Yard, they symbolize the temporal nature of that which we hold dear. They are reminders that change is constant, time is fleeting, and, to quote Neil Young, "Rust never sleeps."

CN 507977

CP 199183

Switchstands from the abandoned CP Owen Sound
Sub, Orangeville, Ontario, July 2, 1999.

Last of the Lake Erie & Northern, July 25, 1991.